THE IT BOOK

CARL JEUNE

THE
IT
BOOK

PALMETTO
PUBLISHING
Charleston, SC
www.PalmettoPublishing.com

The It Book

Copyright © 2024 by Carl Jeune

First Edition

Hardcover ISBN: 979-8-8229-3971-4
Paperback ISBN: 979-8-8229-3972-1

DEDICATION

TO MY FAMILY, I am eternally grateful for the love that fills our hearts and the connection that binds us together. It is a privilege to have you by my side, and I will forever cherish the moments we have shared. My extended family, your love and support have made me feel connected to a larger community. The memories we have created together are treasured, and the bonds we share remain strong, despite the miles that may separate us. Thank you for being my family, my biggest cheerleaders, and my greatest source of love and happiness. I am so fortunate to call you my own.

TO STEPHANI none of this would be possible without your effort and sacrifices

TO MY MOTHER, *VIOLA*,
Sometimes it takes losing someone to truly appreciate and realize their significance in our lives. Losing you made me understand just how much you mean to me. Now that I've found you again, I promise to cherish and value our connection every single day.

CONTENTS

Dedication. v

Introduction ix

The Alpha Male. 1

Who Is a Woman?. 8

Partnership 15

The Spiritual Body. 18

Energy. 22

Vibration. 25

Humanity 28

Color Games 35

How We Got Divided. 38

Education 41

What Did You Say?. 47

Family 57

Money. 62

What Now?. 64

INTRODUCTION

Through the pages of this book, I hope to shed light on the harsh realities that are often overshadowed by the hustle and bustle of day-to-day life. Growing up in the concrete jungle taught me how to navigate the treacherous paths and make difficult choices just to survive. But as I struggled to find my place in this unforgiving world, I realized that there is more to life than mere survival. With each passing day, I learned valuable lessons and gained a deeper understanding of the human experience.

Writing this book has allowed me to reflect on my journey, to explore the depths of my own thoughts and emotions. It is through these words that I hope to bring my experiences to life and make a genuine connection with those who need them the most. In the darkness of the concrete jungle, I discovered a flicker of light. And now, I offer that light to you, dear reader. May this book be a beacon of hope, a source of inspiration, and a guide through the complexities of life.

May every word I write resonate with your soul, reminding you that you are not alone on this journey. Together, we can rise above our circumstances and find meaning amidst the chaos.

Let these pages be a reminder that there is beauty in the struggle, strength in vulnerability, and wisdom in reflection. May my words provide solace in moments of doubt, encouragement in times of despair, and guidance when the path ahead seems unclear. I wrote this book not for myself, but for you. May it be a lifeline, a source of comfort, and a catalyst for change. And as you embark on your own journey, may you find the courage to share your own story, to impact and connect with those who may need it. May the words I write transcend the pages, reaching out to souls in need, reminding them that they, too, have a voice worth sharing.

Throughout the pages, you will come across thought-provoking questions. These queries are designed to make you pause and consider their purpose and relevance in your own life. Delve into these questions and explore how their answers can be applied to your unique circumstances. Use them as opportunities for self-reflection and as catalysts for positive change.

THE ALPHA MALE

...consumed with the need to feel good that we might kill ourselves in the process.

Humans have a natural inclination to label things as it helps them make sense of the world around them. When people have a shared understanding of certain labels, they can effectively convey information and ideas to one another. Labels act as a shorthand that encapsulates meaning and reduces ambiguity, enabling efficient and clear communication. For instance, labels like "apple," "chair," or "book" allow individuals to refer to these objects without having to provide lengthy descriptions each time. Overall, the human need to label things arises from the desire to understand, communicate, remember, and create order in a complex world. When dealing with men and the journey of discovering what makes you a man, I want to first talk about the alpha male label.

If you were to go into a room filled with men and ask how many identify themselves as alpha males, I am almost certain more than half the room will raise their hand. This comes from the belief that the ultimate sign of a man is the alpha male because of what comes with being labeled an alpha male. It's this belief that they are the most successful and powerful male in any group—a strong and successful man who likes to be in charge of others. The alpha male wants to dominate—who you may ask? The alpha male wants to dominate his children, his woman, and other men. He finds strength in making others feel weak.

"Not because he went from
baggin' up them grams to servin' O's
Nah, your daddy was a real nigga,
not 'cause he was hard
Not because he lived a life of crime
and sat behind some bars
Not because he screamed, "Fuck the law"
Although that was true
Your daddy was a real nigga cause he loved you"
—J. Cole

My upbringing starts off in the ghetto of Miami-Dade County. I have traveled to different cities and have been to different neighborhoods, and I've come to the realization that from coast to coast, most ghetto neighborhoods are run similarly. The players and the rules may change a bit but for the most part are about the same. The alpha male label is something that almost every man wants to cling to. In the hood it's not referred to as the alpha male. In street terms it can be referred to as a "real nigga." Most men in the hood want to be labeled an alpha male; they want to be seen as tough; they want to be "a real one." This could be the result of glamorized rap songs, gangster movies, and folklore stories or this could be the result of many falling victim to trying to identify with a label that's not suitable for them to understand the world around them better. For example, I know that a woman and children are not something you dominate. If I want a healthy relationship with anyone, be it women, children, or other men, it has to be a team effort. Seeking to dominate my teammate is not the same as seeking to dominate my opponent.

"The ignorance that make a nigga take his brother life. The bitterness and pain that got him beating on his wife." **—J. Cole**

I grew up wanting to live out the alpha male status which led to me fighting for control over others. Growing up in the environment that I grew up in led to me slowly self-destructing. When I was growing up, you had the term called OGs which stands for Original Gangster. OGs were the ones that were supposed to teach you how to execute the alpha male label. I have come to understand that most of these men were predatorial; they were looking for a young foolish guy like me that would get lost in the fake power that came with the alpha male label and carry out dominating behaviors on their behalf. They themselves were under the alpha male spell, where they were seeking to dominate the younger guys mentally, and the younger guys were carrying out the dominating acts physically. What's ironic to me is that when they are in jail, although they are dominated by a structure that tells them when to eat, when to sleep, when to shower, etc., the whole time while they are incarcerated, they fight to dominate each other. They outnumber the guards and could easily control the situation if they worked together, but due to the dominating structure, the alpha male label is only displayed amongst themselves, and it never crosses their mind to work together.

Friday Movie Scene

The main character Craig is in some trouble, and he goes to grab a gun to protect himself. His father sees him with the gun and he asks him if he feels like a man with that gun, and Craig responds, "I am a man without it."

What does that mean? That he's a man without it? Why did the father ask, "Do you feel like a man with a gun in your hand?"

You would think the OGs would offer game and give tips/tools to the younger generation, but instead they want to dominate a space they feel they have control over. To me, that's just not upright or honorable. That's not what a man is to me. For example, that alpha male label so many young men are looking to obtain, to get validation that they are a man, says that you're not tough if you exhibit emotion. To me, being tough means to possess or exhibit mental, emotional, or physical strength and resilience in challenging or difficult situations. It involves being strong-willed, determined, and having the ability to persevere and stay focused, despite obstacles or adversity. Being tough may also imply being unyielding and able to withstand hardship without giving up or becoming discouraged. It often involves having a courageous and confident attitude and the capacity to handle stress, criticism, or failure while remaining steadfast and pushing through difficult circumstances.

There can be various reasons why men may pretend to be tough. Here are a few possible explanations:

1. Societal Expectations: In many cultures, there is a traditional notion that men should be strong, stoic, and unemotional. Men may feel societal pressure to conform to this ideal of toughness, even if it means suppressing their true emotions or vulnerabilities.

2. Self-Preservation: Men may pretend to be tough as a defense mechanism to protect themselves from potential threats or harm. By projecting an image of strength, they believe they can deter others from targeting or exploiting them.

3. Peer Influence: Male relationships often involve a certain level of competitiveness and social hierar-

chy. Men may pretend to be tough to gain acceptance, fit in, or be seen as dominant within their peer group. It can be a way to maintain their status and avoid being seen as weak or inferior.

4. Emotional Masking: Some men may have grown up in environments where expressing vulnerability or sensitivity was discouraged or even ridiculed. To avoid being judged or rejected, they learn to hide their true emotions behind a tough façade.

5. Fear of Rejection: Men may fear that displaying emotions or admitting weaknesses could make them less desirable to potential romantic partners or friends. They may believe that appearing tough and self-assured makes them more attractive or desirable.

6. Cultural Conditioning: Media, movies, and popular culture often portray tough and rugged men as heroic or admirable figures. Men may be influenced by these portrayals, believing that being tough is an essential characteristic for gaining respect and admiration.

It is crucial to note that not all men pretend to be tough, and these reasons may not be applicable to every individual. People exhibit varied behaviors and characteristics, and it is important to avoid generalizations or stereotypes when discussing gender-specific behaviors.

It is important to recognize that promoting healthy and positive forms of masculinity should involve focusing on empathy, emotional well-being, equality, and respectful relationships, rather than categorizing individuals within rigid hierarchies or labels.

With what has been shared, has anything changed with your viewpoint?

WHO IS A WOMAN?

"The beauty of a woman must be seen from in her eyes, because that is the doorway to her heart, the place where love resides."
—Audrey Hepburn

When discussing who or what is a woman, we must first discuss all of the obstacles plaguing women. I believe once you see everything a woman has had to overcome this will then allow the ability to empathize and connect with what a woman is. I have a strong belief that God is more feminine than we have been made to believe. I believe that the nature of a woman not only carries life but pushes life forward. The woman has endured so much and continues to endure much, but our survival would not be possible without a woman. She is the sacred, holy place of divine creation; her fertile womb is the material wealth of all creation. The seven stages of creation are all created there, she is a fountain of supreme knowledge, wisdom, and intelligence.

The Bible is indeed one of the most influential books in history, shaping the beliefs, values, and cultures of millions of people worldwide. However, it is true that women are often portrayed in a limited or subordinate role throughout the biblical narratives. You can start with Eve eating the fruit, and she is to blame for women suffering through the end of time. Through different characters throughout the Bible such as Jezebel, Zuleikha, Bathsheba, Lot's daughters and Delilah. With this negative imprint of women, do you not see how this could raise nations that devalue what a woman is or truly appreciate their contribution to the world?

Do you know who these women are? Have you thought about how this could negatively impact women today?

The Iroquois Confederacy was under women Indian chiefs' leadership—why do I bring this up? They are responsible for the so-called founding "fathers;" they are the ones that laid down the foundation for the United States constitution as we know it today, but only men get recognized for this achievement. The mainstream recognition often overlooks the contributions of women, not only in relation to the Iroquois Confederacy, but also in general. Recognizing and highlighting their contributions is crucial for a more accurate understanding of history.

Societies often have gender roles and expectations that differentiate women's roles from men's roles. These roles can include stereotypes such as being caregivers, nurturing, or being domestic. Women often face discrimination and inequality in various aspects of life, including employment, education, political representation, and legal rights. Women may also experience gender-based violence and harassment. Women may face societal pressure to conform to certain beauty standards and expectations. This can lead to body image issues, self-esteem concerns, and sometimes unhealthy behaviors. Women often deal with reproductive rights and health-related issues, such as access to contraception, safe abortions, maternal healthcare, and addressing gender-specific health concerns.

Women had to fight for the right to go to school, the right to vote, the right to be outside at night. These are human rights that were denied to the man's counterpart. While all this was going on, what was man's role in all of this?

The Wife Beater Era

The term "wife beater era" refers to a period in history when domestic violence against women was prevalent and socially accepted to some extent. It is important to note that this term is considered derogatory, as it perpetuates negative stereotypes and makes light of a serious issue.

During this era, which can be traced back to the early 20th century, domestic violence was often overlooked or ignored by society, and victims were left without support or legal protection. The term "wife beater" itself originated from a stereotype that portrayed an abusive husband as someone who would physically assault his wife while wearing an undershirt, commonly known as a "wife beater," due to its association with this harmful behavior. In the past, women were often seen as property, with limited legal rights and societal freedom. This power dynamic led to an environment where women faced significant barriers when attempting to escape abusive relationships. Furthermore, law enforcement and legal systems often did not prioritize domestic violence cases, contributing to the acceptance and perpetuation of such abusive behavior.

After facing such afflictions, how do you think the woman would respond?

"To not protect the woman is to not protect the man and vice versa. The man is losing his humanity as long as he denies the woman hers."
—Henry J.

Thankfully, attitudes towards domestic violence have evolved significantly over time. Global movements advocating for women's rights, along with increased awareness and social consciousness, have contributed to changing societal norms and pushing for legal protection for victims of domestic violence. Organizations and initiatives now work to educate, support, and empower survivors of abuse while implementing laws to hold perpetrators accountable for their actions.

The conversation I am trying to have here is that I believe to start to heal, since life starts with a woman, we must first aid the woman—build her up and equip her to return to her natural state, not the current conditions that the world has forced her to become; once she's healthy and full of understanding, she may aid her counterpart and build him up.

There are numerous factors that make it hard for women in society. These include:

1. Gender Bias and Stereotypes: Women often face biases and stereotypes that restrict their opportunities and enforce specific roles and expectations. This includes the assumption that women are more emotional, less competent, or primarily suited for homemaking and child-rearing rather than pursuing careers or leadership positions.

2. Gender Pay Gap: Women generally earn less than men for doing the same job or work of equal value. This pay gap exists across various industries and occupations, reflecting deep-rooted gender inequalities.

3. Lack of Representation and Leadership Positions: Women are underrepresented in politics, corporate leadership positions, and decision-making roles. This limits their influence and ability to shape

policies and decisions that affect their lives and well-being.

4. Unequal Education Opportunities: In some parts of the world, women face barriers to accessing quality education. They may encounter discrimination, limited access to schools or universities, cultural norms that prioritize boys' education over girls', or negative social attitudes towards women's education and empowerment.

5. Gender-based Violence: Women are disproportionately affected by various forms of gender-based violence, including domestic violence, sexual assault, harassment, and trafficking. This not only harms their physical and mental health but also inhibits their ability to participate fully in society.

6. Lack of Maternity Support: Women often face challenges in balancing work and family responsibilities. Limited access to affordable childcare, maternity leave policies that are insufficient or nonexistent, and societal expectations regarding women's primary caregiving role make it difficult for women to advance in their careers or pursue their goals.

7. Cultural and Traditional Norms: In many societies, cultural and traditional norms perpetuate gender inequalities. These norms can restrict women's freedom, limit their choices, and enforce patriarchal power structures that prioritize men's dominance.

8. Political Underrepresentation: Women are often underrepresented in political decision-making bodies, including parliaments and other governing bodies. This leads to policies that may not adequately address women's needs and interests.

9. Objectification and Sexualization: Women are often objectified and their worth reduced to their physical appearance in media, advertising, and popular culture. This perpetuates harmful beauty standards, undermines women's agency, and reinforces gender inequality.

10. Everyday Sexism: Women often experience subtle forms of sexism and discrimination in their daily lives, including catcalling, dismissive attitudes, and double standards. These experiences can undermine women's confidence and limit their opportunities.

PARTNERSHIP

"Darling, you
You give, but you cannot take love."
—Jhené Aiko

There are many psychological and societal factors that can explain why some men struggle to receive love, despite being capable of giving love. It is important to note that these factors do not apply to all men, and individuals can have unique experiences and challenges based on their circumstances, personality traits, and upbringing. Overcoming these difficulties often involves challenging societal expectations, being aware of personal biases and conditioning, and actively working on improving emotional intelligence and communication skills. Therapy, self-reflection, and supportive relationships can also play crucial roles in helping individuals learn to receive love and emotional support.

If you got it all figured out, this is not for you.

I am hoping to share information with the ones that have been affected and are looking for a different perspective. I believe a true man is an awakened, upright individual. We are like the walking dead. When we choose to not deal with issues by getting deep and understanding the inner conflicts we have with ourselves, going to the root to understand why we respond the way that we do to the world around us, we hinder ourselves and those around us. Ask yourself, am I man enough to admit the truth of facts? Seek understanding, then to be understood. Having this lack of knowledge prevents a man from being effective and righteous. A true man understands his need for a woman.

"You know what makes me unhappy?
When brothas make babies
And leave a young mother to be a pappy
And since we all came from a woman
Got our name from a woman
and our game from a woman
I wonder why we take from our women
Why we rape our women
Do we hate our women?
I think it's time to kill for our women
Time to heal our women
be real to our women
And if we don't, we'll have a race of babies
That will hate the ladies
that make the babies

And since a man can't make one
He has no right to tell a woman
when and where to create one
So will the real men get up?"
—Tupac

A true woman is heaven; she's not a slut or a hoe. Her divine strength does not allow her to compromise to any foolishness. When you see any characteristics of a morally less, cheap, sex-starved girl, she is just that: a girl that is not a woman. That is a mentally dead girl who is a victim of this world.

Together, we will create a sanctuary where trust, love, and understanding reign. Women will acknowledge the burdens men bear and assure them that solace can be found within our safe space. We will provide unwavering support and work side by side to achieve common goals. Men will recognize the societal pressures that have devalued women and vow to treat them as equals. They will acknowledge that their own worth is intertwined with the women in their lives, understanding that neglecting or rejecting them is ultimately self-destructive.

In this safe space, we will foster an environment free from judgment and prejudice. We will embrace one another's differences and celebrate our unique contributions. Together, we will build a haven where every individual feels valued, heard, seen, and loved.

THE SPIRITUAL BODY

Is the religion you practice spiritual or ritual?
What does it mean to be spiritual?

Our personal emotions, though valid and important, can sometimes cloud our judgment and prevent us from accepting the truth. It takes courage to set aside our ego and biases and embrace the uncomfortable reality that the truth brings. Moreover, seeking the truth requires a certain level of detachment from our personal emotions. Emotions can be heightened, subjective, and biased, which could lead us astray from objective facts. By acknowledging this and striving to approach the truth with an open mind, we can overcome these personal barriers and gain a deeper understanding of the world.

The truth may not always be pleasant or comforting. It may challenge our beliefs, expose our mistakes, or force us to confront uncomfortable realities. However, it is only by embracing the truth that we can remove the blinders from our eyes and the barriers from our hearts. It is through knowing the truth that we can truly grow and evolve as individuals and as a society.

Let us not allow our personal emotions to hinder our pursuit of truth. Let us be brave enough to confront the discomfort it may bring and open ourselves to the possibilities of growth and understanding. Only then can we become more enlightened, compassionate, and empathetic beings.

When I was younger, I would always have questions about religion but was discouraged about asking them. I was told never to question God; God gave us inquisitive brains so that we could question and learn, but those who are ignorant of the true knowledge of God will discourage you from questioning them because they are fearful of their own ignorance, which shows their inability to legitimately answer your legitimate questions.

In other words, they don't know what they are talking about, so they are scared to answer questions due to ego and pride.

We must always seek and ask questions or we will stop growing in our knowledge. You can't receive any answers of understanding unless you first ask questions of non-understanding. I just don't have this belief or understanding that God would be upset or against you for seeking Him and wanting to understand Him. There are a lot of religious people in the world but not a lot of spiritual people. You must understand this: to be religious doesn't mean spiritual.

There are a lot of people who are religious in practice, but they are not spiritual in their nature.

A religion doesn't automatically make you a spiritual person; a religion just provides you with the blueprint.

To be religious is to habitually practice rituals of a particular religion. I am not here to debate if a religious ritual is good or bad, just pointing out that, in fact, these religious practices are rituals. A ritual doesn't have to be viewed as a negative unless it's used negatively. A particular religious organization's rituals are centered around certain ideas and doctrine. A religious organization of religious ritual aims at attaining spirituality.

We have different religions,
but I believe that there is but one *GOD*.
We have all these different religions,
but they all have the same goal: spirituality.

If we have one goal and one God,
then what are we fighting for?

The path to spirituality is not through division. True spirituality comes from within, through personal self-reflection and a deep connection with the divine. It is not tied to any religious title or name. Unfortunately, some individuals who claim to represent God use their positions to spread hate, prejudice, and intolerance. They create barriers between people of different religions and communities, rather than promoting unity and compassion.

It is essential to recognize these imposters for what they are and not let their actions tarnish the true essence of religion. We must strive to follow the teachings of our faiths that promote love, kindness, and respect for all human beings, regardless of their religious backgrounds. Let us work toward building bridges of understanding and cooperation between different religions and communities, rather than erecting walls of division. Let us strive to be true spiritual beings who embody the values of compassion, forgiveness, and unity.

ENERGY

The body creates energy through the chemical energy process.

In this place of pure energy, we tap into the infinite potential that resides within us. It is the realm where all ideas, thoughts, and possibilities originate. When we open ourselves up to this realm, we transcend the limitations of our conditioned beliefs and expand our perception of what is possible. To access this power, we must create a fertile environment within ourselves. This begins by quieting the mind and letting go of the constant chatter and noise that often dominates our thoughts. Through meditation, mindfulness, or other practices, we create space for a deeper connection with our higher brain.

The higher brain, also known as the intuitive mind or the higher self, holds the key to unlocking our true potential. It is the part of us that is connected to the universal consciousness, where all knowledge and wisdom reside. By tuning into this aspect of ourselves, we can tap into profound insights, inner peace, and boundless creativity. The experience of enlightenment arises when we fully awaken to the power of our higher brain. It is a state of expanded consciousness where we no longer identify solely with our ego or limited beliefs. Instead, we become aware of our interconnectedness with all of existence, experiencing a profound sense of unity and love.

In this state, we can perceive the world from a place of deep understanding and compassion. We are guided by intuition and inner wisdom, making decisions that align with our higher purpose and the greater good. Our creativity flows effortlessly as we tap into the infinite possibilities that exist within the realm of pure energy. Enlightenment is not a destination but rather an ongoing journey of self-discovery and growth. It requires a willingness to let go of old patterns and beliefs that no longer serve us, and to continuously expand our awareness and understanding.

As we embrace the power of the higher brain and cultivate a fertile environment for its expression, we awaken to the limitless potential that resides within us. We tap into the wellspring of pure energy that fuels our transformation and empowers us to create a life of fulfillment, joy, and purpose.

The problem is in our hearts;
our hearts need to be transformed

You may go to church but perhaps you are still searching. There is an empty place in your heart, and something inside tells you that you're not right with God. Nicodemus fasted two days a week. He spent two hours every day in prayer. He tithed, but he was told he must be born again.

Why did Jesus say that Nicodemus must be born again?

To do anything we need an energy source. The body creates energy through the process of a chemical reaction. This is because of the reaction of atoms. All the elements we take into our bodies—oxygen, potassium, calcium, and sodium—have specific charges. When we eat or drink, the molecules break down in our body and work; this process is called cellular respiration. All the things we take into our bodies allow us to have electrical impulses. Electricity is required for the nervous system to send signals throughout the body and to the brain, making it possible for us to move, think, and feel.

If we have this understanding that our body is an energy source, how do you protect your energy?

How do you make sure that your energy exchange is positive?

VIBRATION

"If we accept that sound is vibration and we know that vibration touches every part of our physical being, then we understand that sound is heard not only through our ears but through every cell in our bodies." **—Integrative Oncologist Dr. Mitchell Gaynor**

Vibrational sound therapy can retune your body, mind, and spirit, encouraging relaxation, healing, and wellness.

When you engage in relaxation techniques that involve soothing sounds and vibrations, the effects can reach down to a cellular level within your body. This process helps to restore and enhance the flow of energy, bringing you back toward a state of healthy alignment. Stress, on the other hand, disrupts the natural flow of energy within your body. Initially, it may manifest as a low energy state within your aura, a subtle energetic field that surrounds and interpenetrates your physical body. Over time, if left unaddressed, this disrupted energy flow can contribute to the development of mental and physical illnesses.

Have you ever heard the phrases
'good vibes' and 'bad vibes'?

When our bodies and minds are vibrating at a healthy level, we generally feel well inside and out. When we encounter negative or draining environments or people, our vibrational frequency can be lowered, making us more susceptible to illness and mood issues. However, by utilizing the vibrations and frequencies produced by sound, you can help restore balance and improve overall well-being. For example, clapping hands or strumming a guitar creates vibrations that are transmitted through the air and converted into soundwaves, which the brain interprets as sound.

Vibration really is a keyword.

Sound energy has been used for centuries in various spiritual practices and rituals. It is believed to have the ability to cleanse and purify the soul, allowing for spiritual growth and transformation. Chanting mantras, singing hymns, or practicing sound therapy are some ways in which sound energy is used to tap into the spiritual realm.

Furthermore, sound energy is closely linked to emotions. Certain sounds, such as soothing music or nature sounds, have a calming effect on the mind and can help relieve stress and anxiety. On the other hand, loud, jarring noises can trigger feelings of unease or even anger. This showcases the profound impact sound has on our emotional well-being.

In addition to its effect on the mind and emotions, sound energy also has the potential to heal the body. Sound therapy, also known as sound healing, utilizes vibrations and frequencies to restore balance and harmony within the body. It is believed that certain sounds can stimulate the body's natural healing processes and aid in physical recovery.

The power of sound extends beyond our individual experiences. It is a universal language that transcends cultural and language barriers. Music, for example, has the ability to bring people from different backgrounds together, evoking shared emotions and creating a sense of unity and connection.

However, the power of sound can also be wielded in negative ways. Harsh words, insults, and hateful language have the capacity to hurt and wound others deeply. It is important to be mindful of the words we use and the energy that our speech carries. By choosing to communicate with kindness and compassion, we can create a positive and harmonious environment for ourselves and those around us. Sound energy is a potent force that is intricately connected to our consciousness and spirituality. It has the power to influence our emotions, heal our bodies, and connect us with others. We must recognize and respect its immense power, using it wisely and with intention.

HUMANITY

There's no hotline to dial to say the world needs help.

Before the civil war, psychiatrists diagnosed slaves with what they called drapetomania: a mental illness in which the slave possessed an irrational desire for freedom and tendency to try to escape.

Could you believe that someone once said you have a mental illness because you have a desire to want human rights and the freedom to exist?

Some "experts" diagnosed slaves with a mental illness simply because they yearned for freedom and attempted to escape their oppressive conditions. This misguided perspective reflects the deeply ingrained prejudice and injustice prevalent during that time period.

This Black and White Thing

I find no pleasure in doing this, and I am aware that it is inappropriate and unproductive to diagnose or label an entire racial group, including white people, based on a specific historical context. I am also aware that when you put something like this under a microscope you should examine the socio-cultural, economic, and political factors that influenced the behaviors, attitudes, and beliefs of people during that time period. But for the sake of addressing this black and white issue, I think it will help me paint the picture that I want to paint. We just discussed how they came out with a mental illness describing black slaves during that time. I thought I would diagnose the white people during that time to highlight how irresponsible and insensitive this can be.

The diagnosis: *Antisocial personality disorder*

This is a mental health condition characterized by a pervasive pattern of disregard for and violation of the rights of others. Those with this condition often engage in manipulative, deceitful, and irresponsible behavior without feeling remorse or empathy for the harm they cause to others.

They have difficulty understanding and relating to the feelings and experiences of others. They may disregard the needs, feelings, and rights of others, leading to a disregard for societal norms. People with this disorder often act impulsively without considering the consequences of their actions. They may engage in criminal activities. They may lie, manipulate, or exploit others for personal gain without feeling guilty or remorseful. They may engage in aggressive behaviors, such as bullying, physical fights. They have little to no remorse or guilt for the harm they cause to others. They may rationalize their behavior or blame others to avoid taking responsibility for their actions.

Let's look at the programming of all the slave books, movies, and documentaries the government, schools, and media have shown you over your lifetime. Wouldn't the white people they depreciate during these times fit the mental illness? You want to know what's the worst part about all of this? Through time this behavior, this psychosis, has never been addressed because people are afraid to say the hard things, to look in the mirror, and call it like it is!

It runs deep—they do not trust *white* people.

It is important to recognize that generalizations about any racial or ethnic group are not accurate or fair. It is not accurate to say that all black people hate white people, just as it is not accurate to claim that all white people harbor negative attitudes toward black people. Individuals' beliefs and attitudes are shaped by a multitude of factors, including personal experiences, upbringing, and social influences. However, like any other diverse group, including white people, there may be individuals within the black community who hold negative or prejudiced views toward people of other races, including the white community. It is essential to understand that these individuals do not represent the beliefs of all black people.

For a moment, I will play devil's advocate, I want to examine this idea that *Black* people hate *white* people, and when I say this, I want you to ask the question: Could you blame them for hating *white* people? I mean, can you truly disagree that a *black* person hating a *white* person is a bad thing? I think the opposite: I find it foolish for a *black* person to not hate a *white* person. I am a God-fearing man, and I know you have been taught that you should not hate, so I want to remove myself and ideas. I want to hate what God hates, and you know what I have come to find out?

Below are God's instructions. If you are to follow his ways, to be a reflection of Him, you should hate these things as well:

- Proverbs 16:5
  - » Prideful person

- Proverbs 6:16–19
  - » a lying tongue
  - » hands that shed innocent blood
  - » a heart that devises wicked schemes
  - » feet that are quick to rush into evil
  - » a false witness who pours out lies
  - » a person who stirs up conflict in the community

So as a *black* person going through slavery knowing what God hates, how could it be that you not hate a *white* person? (I am not saying to hate anyone, simply asking to digest this train of thought.)It's like someone putting their foot on your neck, choking you out, and you in turn say I cannot hate this person because...

"If a black man has to be responsible for every day of his life for something that he did not do, that he has to pay for the history, for the color of his skin, white people must pay as well. The great pain is that you cannot get across to the white person that you as human as he is."
—James Baldwin

We had a time period where there were laws that:

- banned against a slave owning a weapon.
- banned a black person from testifying against a white person in court.
- prevented blacks from owning drums or horn instruments.
- prohibited blacks from taking part in any kind of trade.
- in New York, three or more black people were refused meeting up at once.

And if we are being honest, it's still going on today, just in different forms.

Even when you converted into a Christian, that conversion would not change your slave status. Law enforcement was given the authority to search and whip slaves if they appear to have disorderly behavior.

There are more black males than females born in the United States; however, by the time the two reach eighteen, when factoring in incarceration, homicide, suicide, black females outnumber black males seven to one. The black males are effectively dying at the rate of endangered species.

Now I know at this time I might have triggered a few people or made them feel uncomfortable, but when I am throwing out shades of color, black/white, I want you to think: why are you uncomfortable?

I know the answer is because you identify with one of these groups. Whether black or white. One side being black saying, "I am black, and I don't want to hate anyone." The other side being white and you are saying, "I do not want to be hated." I want to say both of you are right; however, you're looking at things in the wrong way. You separated yourself black and white off of the color or your skin. You fell right into the trap to think that you are different because your paint jobs are different. It is not as if blacks are from Mars and whites are from Pluto. All humans, regardless of race, religion, or background, share a common origin. It is essential to recognize and appreciate our shared humanity.

It is also important to acknowledge the historical and social factors that have led to the division and discrimination we see today. Throughout history, humans have constructed systems of power and privilege that have marginalized certain groups, based on characteristics such as race, ethnicity, and religion. Understanding and confronting these systems of inequality must be an ongoing process. It requires education, empathy, open-mindedness, and a willingness to challenge our own biases and prejudices. It is crucial to listen to the experiences and perspectives of others and work towards creating a more just and inclusive society for everyone. By promoting understanding and embracing diversity, we can strive to dismantle the barriers that separate us and build a world where everyone is valued and respected.

COLOR GAMES

Cry Freedom movie, court scene:
Why do you call yourself black?
You look more brown than black.

Steve Biko: *Why do you call yourselves white?*
You look more pink than white.

Those in power have been using various tactics to keep people divided and hurt throughout history. Here are some common tricks they have employed:

1. Divide and conquer: This strategy involves creating divisions and animosities among different groups within society, such as along ethnic, religious, or socioeconomic lines. By pitting these groups against each other, those in power can distract people from their shared grievances and maintain control.

2. Propaganda and disinformation: Manipulating information and spreading propaganda is a sig-

nificant tool for those in power to control public opinion. They can disseminate false narratives that demonize and dehumanize specific groups, leading to heightened tensions and further division.

3. Creating scapegoats: By targeting certain individuals or groups as the cause of societal problems, those in power can divert attention from their own failures and injustices. Blaming a particular group for issues such as economic inequality or political instability creates division and fosters resentment toward the scapegoated group.

4. Suppressing dissent: Those in power often employ tactics to silence and marginalize critics and opposition. By limiting freedom of speech, assembly, or the press, they can control the dissemination of alternative perspectives and discourage collective action against their rule.

5. Exploiting identity politics: Manipulating identity-based issues and using them as political tools can polarize communities and pit different groups against each other. By stoking fear, anger, or resentment around identity markers such as race, religion, or gender, those in power can maintain divisive power dynamics.

6. Promoting economic inequality: A society with significant income and wealth disparities inherently perpetuates divisions. By favoring policies that concentrate wealth and power in the hands of a few,

those in power can create environments of social unrest and perpetuate divisions between the privileged and the marginalized.

There is in fact but one race, of many colors.

HOW WE GOT DIVIDED

no church in the wild

The titles Black American and African American are fake, inappropriate European titles, created to keep indigenous people (aka Indian) of the western hemisphere (the Americas) under a spell of ignorance. "Black American" and "African American" implies that African Americans are only connected to America and Africa, but they are not African nor have any connection to Africa, and they are accepted in America only as second class. They have been stripped of their true indigenous identity. This can lead to a psychological and spiritual disconnect because they cannot connect to their heritage. For example, Jesse Jackson, a South Carolina Cherokee Indian, started to promote the fake title of African American that has been imposed upon black Indians, indigenous to the western hemisphere.

What law did Virginia pass in 1705?
What was the Virginia weapons law in 1723?

In 1705, Virginia passed the Virginia Slave Code, also known as "An Act Concerning Servants and Slaves." This law defined the legal status and treatment of enslaved black Indians and their descendants, establishing a system of chattel slavery in the colony. It restricted the rights and freedoms of enslaved people, denying them basic human rights, and ensuring their owners had complete control over their lives and labor. The Virginia Slave Code set a precedent for future slave laws in other colonies and states.

European powers sought to establish dominance and exploit resources in other parts of the world. This often involved the subjugation and control of indigenous populations. In order to justify this domination, Europeans developed ideologies of racial superiority which considered people of European descent as superior to those of other races. During this period Europeans (Whites) were given guns and food and rights to vote, while others were stripped of their rights.

The reason for this was because together the Europeans (Whites) and the Indians (Blacks) outnumbered the people in charge of power structure. After the Bacon rebellion, the Europeans were not given the ability to move up in class, so the idea was to give them something else, and what they gave them was power over another group of people; so they sold them the idea of a "white identity." This was done to reinforce the belief in the inherent superiority of Europeans. By creating a concept of whiteness, Europeans attempted to create a sense of unity and social cohesion among themselves, while excluding people of color from the same privileges and rights.

This system of racial hierarchy created significant disparities in power, wealth, and social status. It entrenched prejudices and discrimination, leading to the marginalization and oppression of non-white populations. Over time, these racial divisions have had far-reaching consequences, having shaped social, economic, and political structures in numerous societies.

Did you know before the Bacon rebellion, the term white or black to describe a person was not ever used? Do you now see the impact that this had on how we live today?

EDUCATION

Once your kids start school they will be in school more than they are at home.

The industrial age was good for America/bad for American people.

We made a switch as a society from hunter-gatherers to agricultural and then to the industrial age and now in technology. The earliest human beings didn't need schools to pass along information. They educated youngsters on an individual basis within the family unit. Over time, however, populations grew, and societies formed. Rather than every family being individually responsible for education, people soon figured out that it would be easier and more efficient to have a small group of adults teach a larger group of children. In this way, the concept of the school was born. Ancient schools weren't like the schools we know today, though. The earliest schools often focused more on teaching skills and passing along religious values, rather than teaching specific subject areas as is common today.

In the United States, the first school was the Boston Latin School, which was founded in 1635. It was the first public school and the oldest existing school in the country. The earliest schools focused on reading, writing, and mathematics. The New England colonies led the way in requiring towns to set up schools. The Massachusetts Bay Colony made basic education a requirement in 1642. However, many of the earliest schools were only for boys, and there were usually few, if any, options for girls.

In 1833, the government passed the Factory Act, making two hours of education a day compulsory for children working in factories. The government also granted money to charities for schools for the first time. The moment that money began to influence the education system it led us down the wrong path. One could assume the decision to grant money to charities for schools was likely a response to the growing concern for improving access to education for the working class. By providing financial support to charities, the government aimed to expand educational opportunities and bridge the gap between the privileged and underprivileged. However, introducing money into the education system created risks. The influence of money and the potential for corruption led to the prioritization of profit over quality education. This resulted in ill-equipped teachers, inadequate resources, and a focus on monetary gains rather than the holistic development of students.

During the industrial age, the school was designed to get people equipped and prepared for the workforce, which was mostly factory work during that time. The designs of the classroom were set up like an assembly line because it was supposed to prepare the students for their jobs in the factories. Unfortunately, we are still following this model even though times have changed. The school system has not. The habits we pick up in school no longer create economic value. In fact, we may be learning to destroy value. There is a saying that knowledge is power, but there is little to no value in education in America. Many students take an entitlement stance because it is offered for "free." The concepts of what it costs to run a school are lost because students are so frustrated with the school environment; they don't even have room to care. That's the biggest obstacle; they lost the desire to be in school.

The credit for our modern version of the school system usually goes to Horace Mann. When he became Secretary of Education in Massachusetts in 1837, he set forth his vision for a system of professional teachers who would teach students an organized curriculum of basic content. By 1918, every state required students to complete elementary school. Educational improvements grew by leaps and bounds during the 20th century, leading to the advanced systems we have today. After the American Revolution, education became a higher priority. States quickly began to establish public schools. School systems were not uniform, however, and would often vary greatly from state to state.

The two major ideas that should be taught to children of every country are:

1. The value of the individual
2. The fact of one humanity

There are three duties of education:

- The first effort for education to civilize the child is to train and rightly direct his instincts.
- The second obligation is to be able to bring about the child's true culture (not the history of who won the war), training him to use his intellect rightly.
- The third duty of education is to bring out and to develop intuition.

When these three are developed and functioning, you will have a civilized, cultured, and spiritually awakened human being; a person will then be instinctively correct and intellectually sound and intuitively aware. Their souls, their minds, and their brains will be functioning as the should and in right relation to each other, thus again producing coordination and correct alignment.

1. An atmosphere of love: Where fear is cast out and the child realizes he has no cause of shyness or caution. The child receives respectful treatment from others and is expected to also give respectful treatment to others in return. Love always draws forth what is best in a child.
2. An atmosphere of patience: The child can become normally and naturally a seeker after knowledge; the child is always met with a careful response to

questions, and there is not a sense of speed or hurry (opposite of what happens when trying to prepare a student for a standardized test).

3. An atmosphere of ordered activity: Where the child can learn the first principles of responsibility. When the child is developing a sense of responsibility, it will factor in determining a child's character and future career.

4. An atmosphere of understanding: Where a child is always sure of the reason and motives for his actions, although we may not always approve of what the child has done. It is always the older generation that fosters in a child an early and unnecessary guilt of wrongdoing. Much importance is laid upon petty things that are not really wrong, but annoying to parents or teachers. The true sense is not recognized for what it is, failure to understand the child. If these aspects of the child's life are handled right, then true wrong things, the violation of others, the hurting and damaging others in order to achieve personal gain, will emerge in the right attitude and at the right time.

A better education system should prioritize teaching empathy and understanding to students. By incorporating empathy training into the curriculum, students can learn to put themselves in others' shoes, understand different perspectives, and appreciate diversity. This will help break down barriers and reduce prejudices by promoting a more compassionate and inclusive society. The curriculum should include lessons that challenge and debunk stereotypes and prejudices. Education should provide accurate and balanced information about different cultures, races, religions, genders, and socioeconomic backgrounds. By addressing biases and misconceptions head-on, students can develop a more open-minded and accepting mindset. The education system should promote collaboration, teamwork, and communication skills. These skills are crucial for fostering understanding and building harmonious relationships with others.

By incorporating these values into the curriculum, promoting cultural exchanges, and developing teachers' cultural competence, we can break down barriers, remove prejudices, and raise a new generation capable of living in harmony and goodwill with others.

WHAT DID YOU SAY?

We once all spoke one language; a time when we were connected with the world around us. During this era, communication flowed effortlessly between individuals, tribes, and cultures, transcending boundaries, and fostering unity. People shared stories, knowledge, and experiences, enabling them to understand and empathize with one another. This common language served as a powerful tool for cooperation and collaboration in the pursuit of collective goals. People could work together seamlessly, harnessing their combined strengths and talents to build prosperous communities and advance their societies. The world was a vibrant tapestry of diverse cultures, all interconnected through this shared language.

The benefits of this shared language extended beyond interpersonal communication. It facilitated the exchange of ideas, innovations, and scientific advancements. With a common language, discoveries made in one part of the world could be shared and built upon by others, sparking a rapid acceleration of progress and development. Moreover, this shared language fostered a deep connection to the natural world. People understood their interconnectedness with nature, recognizing the importance of stewardship and living in harmony with the environment. This wisdom was passed down through generations, ensuring the preservation of ecosystems and biodiversity.

However, as time went on, the unity and interconnectedness began to erode. The proliferation of different languages and the resulting linguistic barriers led to misunderstandings and divisions. Cultural differences became increasingly highlighted and emphasized, creating a sense of "us versus them" mentality. Today, we exist in a world fragmented by numerous languages, each with its unique cultural nuances and barriers. This linguistic diversity enriches our global tapestry, but it also presents challenges in communication and understanding.

Nonetheless, the remnants of that once-shared language can still be observed in certain universal aspects of human expression, like music, art, and emotions. These bridges offer glimpses of our shared humanity, reminding us that despite our linguistic differences, we are all interconnected and part of a larger global family. As we navigate this evolving world, it is crucial to remember the power of language as a means of connection and understanding.

Why does this matter? How does this impact how students learn today?

Do you understand how insensitive it is to mock a child coming from the inner city, speaking "Hood English" or Spanglish? That is an attack on their culture.

Cultural diversity and language variations are essential aspects of our society, and we should encourage understanding and appreciation rather than ridicule. Education plays a crucial role in ensuring effective communication skills. It is important to teach children the appropriate context and register for different situations, including when to use more formal or standardized English. However, it is equally important to respect and acknowledge the various forms of language and dialects spoken within different communities. Promoting inclusivity, providing support, and encouraging language development without belittling or attacking any cultural background should be the goal.

Love

Love must be practical, tested manifestation, and not just theory or just an idea and a pleasing sentiment. It is something that has grown in the trials and tests of life. Love for many people is not really love but a mixture of desire to love and the desire to be loved, plus the willingness to do anything to show and evoke this sentiment. Love is not a sentiment or an emotion, nor is it desire or a selfish motive for right actions in daily life. Love is a force that leads to unity and inclusiveness; it's an action. Love is hard; it is a challenge; it's a difficult thing to apply to all conditions of life and its expression; it will demand the utmost you have to give; it removes your selfish personal tendencies/activities.

To know love is to know pain. If you search and understand the power that is in dealing with pain, you may then also open the door for you to understand love. Pain is the cold of isolation which leads to the warmth of the sun; pain is getting burned and finally knowing/appreciating the coolness of water. Pain is stepping out in the world, getting chewed up and spit out, and love is coming back into a welcoming home. Pain leads the human soul out of darkness into light, out of bondage into liberation, out of agony into peace.

Animals suffer physically and sentiently. A person suffers physically, sentiently, and also mentally. Mental suffering is due to aspects in the lower mind such as anticipation, memory, imagination, remorse, and the inherent urge to be accepted, which brings the sense of loss and failure. We seek to avoid pain, but it is the protector of substance. It warns you of danger. It is this process, related to the soul defining itself with substance, when pain, disease, and death lose their hold on a person. The soul no longer subjected to these requirements and now at this point you are free. Pain is not something you should run from; it is a purifier when address and met properly.

We talked about pain, we talked about love, and as you go through this thing called life, you will be hurt by both.

Love and pain come with hurt, so let's talk about healing. Healing comes from knowledge. When entering the world of healing, you must come with the intention to gain knowledge and apply it. When someone comes to the state of truly open-mindedness and is ready to accept new information and theories, they discover the old and dearly held truth is not lost but only regulated to its rightful place in a larger scheme. It's like watching from a different perspective. It makes you more powerful because now you can see things from a wide range. For example, in my background in playing football, there is this famous saying: The eye in the sky does not lie. A coach on the field may see something one way, the player playing may see it in a different way, but when you go look at it from the person recording and getting all the angles, you gain more knowledge of the situation; you can see it better and do better. One must seek and want to do better for themselves if they want to heal. As discussed earlier we are spiritual beings, high energy people.

The self-will and energy that individuals release in their quest for healing have immense power to bring about their own healing. By nurturing the forces they desire to utilize, they can harness the potential to transform their physical, emotional, and spiritual well-being. To effectively channel these healing energies, individuals must cultivate discipline and control over their appetites. This includes not only dietary choices but also the thoughts and emotions they indulge in. By building a clean body, free from toxins and negative influences, they create a conducive environment for the easy flow of healing forces through their own being and to others.

By adopting a disciplined approach and creating clear channels, individuals can tap into the self-will and release energy that brings about healing on multiple levels. This involves actively engaging in practices like meditation, mindfulness, healthy eating, regular exercise, and self-reflection. Through these practices, individuals can cultivate a higher state of consciousness that facilitates the healing process.

Love prescription
In love is a temporary emotional high,
and you need to pursue real love.

Being in love gives you an illusion that you're in an intimate relationship, where you feel you belong to each other. "I would do anything to make you happy." We believe that he/she will be committed to meeting our needs, that he/she loves us as much as we love him/her, and that he/she would never do anything to hurt us. That thinking is always fanciful. We become blind to the fact that everyone has their own flaws, insecurities, and selfish tendencies. This illusion of love can lead to disappointment and heartbreak when we realize that our partner is not perfect and cannot fulfill all of our expectations. We may start to question their love for us, feeling betrayed and hurt when they act in ways that go against our idealized image of them.

It is important to recognize that love is not a fairy tale; it requires effort, compromise, and acceptance of each other's imperfections. Realizing that both individuals in a relationship are egocentric beings with their own needs and desires allows for a more realistic and grounded approach to love. Instead of expecting our partner to always put us first and never hurt us, we should strive for open communication, understanding, and mutual growth. By acknowledging our own egocentric nature and that of our partner, we can foster a healthier and more balanced relationship based on empathy, compromise, and realistic expectations.

Talk to me nice!

No one has ever hurt you; it is the way that you look at life; it comes from your programing. A person cannot understand you or be there for you if they don't understand how you see the world. I am aware of the importance that external factors and the actions of others can cause, but we are here to discuss how you take control of your life. You begin working on yourself first.

Our outlook and perceptions can shape our experiences in life. If we have a negative or distorted view of the world, it can impact how we interpret and respond to situations.

While our personal perspective plays a significant role in how we navigate life, it does not negate the possibility of others causing us pain.

He cheats & it hurts...
A wise person can play a fool,
but a fool can't play wise.

If you are able to change your conditional wiring and understand that he didn't cheat on you, he just cheats. It's the perspective or a realization that cheating is not specific to you or your relationship. It's the understanding that the actions are not a reflection of your worth or a result of something lacking in your relationship, but rather a pattern of behavior that the other person engages in regardless of the circumstances.

If it hurts, it is about you trying to fix something unfixable or unwilling to change. It's the idea that if you choose to be in a relationship with someone who has a history of cheating or does not have a moral code, that it's wrong; you should not be surprised or hurt when they continue to cheat. It is the individual's own responsibility to choose someone who aligns with their values and expectations in order to avoid pain and disappointment. Cheating reflects the cheater's character rather than a personal attack on the person they are in a relationship with. Therefore, the onus is on the individual to make these choices wisely and be aware of the consequences.

It's the emotional punishment you give yourself for someone else's behavior. That was not your issue, but you took it as your issue.

Building relationships requires time, effort, and careful consideration. It is crucial to understand the person you are getting involved with before fully committing and allowing them into your life. By doing so, you take on the responsibility of who enters your world, knowing that once someone is a part of your life, you cannot control their actions or decisions.

Learning the person you are giving yourself to involves various aspects, such as understanding their values, beliefs, and goals. It means being attentive to their behavior, observing how they treat others, and assessing their compatibility with your own principles. It requires patience and curiosity to explore their interests, past experiences, and motivations. By investing time in this process, you can gain insight into their character, integrity, and overall suitability as a partner, friend, or any other role they might play in your life.

Taking responsibility for who you allow into your world is vital, because the people we surround ourselves with have a significant impact on our well-being and personal growth. Their words, actions, and energy can influence our emotions, attitudes, and even our own behavior. Therefore, it is essential to evaluate whether someone aligns with our values and supports our personal development.

While it is impossible to control others once they are in our life, we can pave the way for healthy relationships by setting boundaries and expressing our expectations. Communicating openly and honestly about our needs, desires, and concerns can foster understanding and create a foundation of trust. However, it is important to recognize that each individual is ultimately responsible for their own thoughts, choices, and actions.

It is crucial to take your time and learn about the person you are allowing into your life. By taking on the responsibility of who enters your world, you can make more informed decisions and surround yourself with individuals who are compatible with your values, goals, and overall well-being. Remember that while you cannot control others, open communication and setting boundaries can contribute to healthy relationships.

FAMILY

The family unit serves as the foundational building block of society.

The importance of the family unit in society cannot be overstated. Family is the first source of socialization for individuals. From an early age, children learn societal norms, values, and moral principles within the family. This contributes to their overall development and helps shape their character and behavior. Family provides emotional support and acts as a safety net. Members of the family can rely on each other during times of joy, sorrow, stress, or crisis. This support system promotes mental and emotional well-being, which is crucial for individuals to flourish in society. It is a place where individuals feel safe and protected. This stability creates a sense of belonging, which promotes healthier relationships and a stronger sense of identity.

The family unit influences physical health and overall well-being. Healthy habits, such as proper nutrition, exercise, and self-care are often reinforced within the family. Additionally, family members provide emotional and caregiving support during illness or times of poor health. Families are also vital for the transmission of cultural values, traditions, and heritage. Through generations, families pass down customs, cultural practices, and important stories that connect individuals to their roots and help foster a sense of identity. Strong families contribute to the social fabric, promoting stability, resilience, and overall well-being within the larger community.

Change is inevitable.

Change is necessary for the survival and growth of any entity, including the family unit. As society evolves, so do the circumstances, challenges, and expectations faced by families. Adapting to these changes and understanding the need for transformation is vital for the family unit to thrive.

The Wire TV series

Preston 'Bodie' Broadus: "And then I'm standing here like an asshole, holding my Charles Dickens 'cause I ain't got no muscle, no backup. Shit man, yo, if this was the old days..."

Slim Charles: "Yeah now, well, the thing about the old days...they the old days."

One crucial factor driving the need for change in the family unit is the shifting dynamics of gender roles and expectations. Traditional gender roles, where men were typically the breadwinners, while women took care of the household and children, have significantly evolved. Today, families are becoming more egalitarian, with both partners sharing responsibilities and contributing to the financial well-being of the household. Embracing this change can lead to greater partnership and harmony within the family.

Relationships between men and women are suffering in a major way.

The historical struggles between men and women, where power dynamics have caused harm and oppression, have had a significant impact on the advancement of gender equality. The feminist movement sought to address these imbalances, but sometimes, when previously oppressed groups come into power, they repeat the same patterns. Sexism and racism are both forms of discrimination and prejudice, but they manifest in different ways and have distinct historical and social contexts.

This cycle creates division and dehumanization, ultimately hurting everyone involved. The key is to acknowledge past failures, understand their impact on both men and women, and work together to build a more equal and unified society. Breaking it down to my sports background, when it's playoff time and you go on a run to try to win a championship, ego has to go out the window. One game this guy may have an amazing game, and the next game, the other team works to shut him down. That's when someone else has an opportunity to have a good game. This analogy of teamwork in sports emphasizes the importance of setting aside personal egos and working collaboratively within the family unit to raise children who are prepared to challenge the harsh world they are going to have to live in.

No one follows a fool unless they are fools themselves.

Although it's in man's nature to naturally be aggressive because men have a high level of testosterone, you cannot misuse your nature. Being a man does not inherently mean dominating over something or someone. Masculinity can be defined in various ways and should not be limited to aggression or dominance. Being a man can involve qualities such as empathy, compassion, and nurturing, which are equally important for personal growth and building healthy relationships. True leadership and guidance are not about forcing one's authority but rather about serving the needs of others. Effective leadership requires responsibility, knowledge, and wisdom, which can be developed through experience, education, and self-reflection.

Men can support women's rights by advocating for equal opportunities for women in all areas of life, including education, employment, and leadership positions. This includes actively listening to women's voices, supporting their ideas and initiatives, and challenging any form of discrimination or harassment. By embracing a more holistic under-standing of masculinity, men can contribute to a more equal and just society for everyone.

The world puts this oppression on women they sexual-ize and stripped down to being brainless, and thoughtless. I don't find it wise to associate with any of these negative characteristics! I want to point out that a lot of women have played into the male chauvinism as a way of sitting back and taking very little initiative to develop their own po-tential, and just want to live off a man like a leech. If you operate in that manner, your lack of motivation and inspi-ration is just as poor as the egotistical male you choose as your partner that is oppressing you. To just want someone to take you, and you are a grown adult, is counterproduc-tive. I encourage women to develop their own potential and build together with their partners, rather than relying solely on them for survival.

MONEY

If the hood is so poor, explain gentrification

Don't you find it crazy that someone could live in the hood, and because of the daily violence, the struggle, they truly believe that they are poor? At the same time, someone else comes up with a great idea and says this would be a great spot to have a spa or a coffee shop. Due to the daily exposure to violence and struggling conditions in an impoverished area, it creates a mindset where individuals believe that poverty is the only reality for them.

However, great ideas and opportunities can arise from any situation, even in areas facing difficulties. The potential for development and improvement exists in all communities, regardless of their current state. It is important to provide support, resources, and opportunities to uplift communities and empower individuals to break free from the cycle of poverty and violence.

One man's trash is another man's treasure.

This thing is all about perception. I am challenging young people to look at their community as something to be proud of. I know growing up in chaos and poverty makes it hard, and that often the goal is to "make it out" of those circumstances. However, remember that someone from outside the community sees the potential and value that you don't recognize. There are untapped opportunities and resources within your community you should appreciate and take advantage of.

American citizens have become spoiled and lazy. I believe that we have one of the highest levels of poverty. What I mean by that is when you compare a poor person in Dubai to a poor person in Liberty City or a poor person in Columbia to a poor person on the southside of Houston, you will quickly see that many of the poor people in America have poor minds that create poor habits, but they are not poor. They wear designer clothes, have nice cars, and have the opportunity to attend school for free. The poor people in America spend more than people in poverty in other countries, and that it's not just about how much money you make or save but how you manage your finances. What I am trying to highlight is the need for financial education and awareness among low-income communities, because the money is there; they just don't believe it because of what they see day to day.

WHAT NOW?

*The lost art of teaching how to think,
not what to think, needs to be revived.
Born ignorant—not stupid.*

We come into this world without any preconceived notions or biases. We are like a blank slate, ready to absorb and learn from our surroundings. However, as we grow older and more influenced by society, we start to develop certain beliefs and perspectives. We are taught to see things from one side, whether it be through education, media, or cultural norms.

The problem with this is that it limits our understanding and prevents us from gaining a more comprehensive view of the world. We become trapped in a narrow mindset, unable to see beyond our own limited perspectives. Ignorance arises when we fail to acknowledge and challenge these preconceptions. To combat ignorance, we need to actively seek new experiences and learn from them. Life itself becomes our greatest teacher. Through interactions with different people, exposure to new cultures, exploration of various ideas, and continuous learning, we can broaden our horizons and overcome the limitations imposed by our learned biases.

Questioning the doctrines and teachings that we have been exposed to is crucial to breaking free from ignorance. It is through critical thinking and open-mindedness that we can challenge the beliefs that have been ingrained within us. We should not accept everything at face value but instead, constantly question, analyze, and re-evaluate what we have been taught.

We must organize, strengthen ourselves and our communities.

- buy collectively as a group
- protect our women and children
- create avenues for more doctors, lawyers, judges, teachers, coaches, police men
- protect and build up one another
- educate our own
- look for every opportunity to start a business, servicing the needs of people

Here are some ideas for how young individuals can uplift their neighborhoods:

1. Volunteer: Encourage them to become active volunteers in local organizations or initiatives. They can support local schools, community centers, or

nonprofit organizations that work towards community development.

2. Mentorship: Encourage them to share their skills and knowledge with younger kids by becoming mentors or tutors. This can help inspire and empower the next generation.

3. Organize cleanup events: They can take the initiative to organize cleanup campaigns in their neighborhoods to improve its appearance and promote cleanliness.

4. Start community gardens: Encourage them to transform vacant lots into green spaces where community members can come together, grow their own food, and learn about sustainable practices.

5. Advocate for change: Encourage them to join or start youth organizations that address social issues and advocate for positive changes within their community.

6. Entrepreneurship: Support and mentor young entrepreneurs who are interested in starting their own businesses. This can create economic opportunities within the community while keeping young people engaged and invested in their neighborhood.

By doing these things, we can improve the overall well-being and empowerment of our community. When we organize and come together, we can amplify our voices and push for positive change. By collectively buying goods and services, we can support local businesses and create economic opportunities within our community. It is crucial to protect our women and children, as they are often more vulnerable to various forms of violence and discrimination. By creating avenues for professions such as doctors, lawyers, judges, teachers, coaches, and police officers within our community, we can ensure that our people have access to essential services and representation. Building each other up and providing education for our own community members can lead to a stronger and more self-sufficient community. Lastly, starting businesses that cater to the needs of our people can generate both economic growth and job opportunities within our community.

Milton Keynes UK
Ingram Content Group UK Ltd.
UKHW020750250224
438339UK00015B/100/J